I0224799

Ready to Be Thirty!

Antionette Turner

Copyright © 2020 Antionette Turner.

All rights reserved. Printed in the United States of America.
No part of this publication may be reproduced, stored in a
retrieval system, or transmitted in any form or by any means,
electronic, mechanical, photocopying, recording, or
otherwise, without the written permission of the publisher.

ISBN: 978-1-951838-13-3

Portions of this book are works of nonfiction. Certain names
and identifying characteristics have been changed.

Publisher: 90 Day Legacy Builders

Table of Contents

Dedication i

Acknowledgements ii

Chapter One 1

Chapter Two 8

Chapter Three 15

Chapter Four 20

Chapter Five 28

Chapter Six 35

Chapter Seven 43

Chapter Eight 51

Chapter Nine 59

Last Chapter 64

Dedication

This book is dedicated to my family. Everything I do, I do with you all in mind: know that, understand that, trust that, and believe that. This is the end of any generational curse we have. This is the start of generational wealth. I claim all great things for us, through us, and by us. We deserve and we will receive. It's our time. We gone be alright! God has covered us with His blood and He will continue to do so. I got us. There is nothing we can't get through together! Thank you for believing in me and for believing in yourselves enough to keep pushing forward. I love you all, forever.

Acknowledgements

To the person that motivated me to write this book, thank you. You know who you are. You encouraged me to create generational wealth. You sparked a light in me that I didn't know would be lit so soon. You taught me how to manifest and made me understand that I was already walking in my purpose. You helped me realize that I was more dope than I could fathom. So, thank you for those long, in-depth, and intellectual conversations that made me take it there and kept me going. Thank you for helping me refocus when I got off track. Thank you for believing in me more than I believed in myself. No matter what has transpired, I will forever be thankful that God placed you in my life. Thank you for pouring into me what God needed you to.

Thank you to my best friends Sha'Net, Troy and Destiny. College has a way of bringing people together for a lifetime. I am glad that I was blessed with friends like you all. There is constant support, encouragement, and nonstop motivation. The flow of great energy and amazing vibes has been ongoing since day one. We never let each other slack. I don't know what I would do without you guys. I love you all: now and always. Thank you for being such amazing, true, and unconditional friends.

Thank you to each and every person who played a role in my life whether it was big, small, positive, or negative. Whatever it was, it mattered and it was needed in order for me to become who I am today. Thank you. You are deeply and greatly appreciated!

Chapter One

Dirty Thirty

Everyone looks to turning thirty as this big, horrible thing. Once you turn thirty, you are old as hell and dusty. Your life is halfway over (depending on your ethnic background). You are not "young and popping" anymore because you've reached that godforsaken age. Of course, that's according to society and an immature mindset. Low and behold, you are a single woman with no kids or a man whose business has not yet hit the roof. That's most people's perception of life. No one is ready to hit that "Dirty Thirty." It all falls back to your state of mind.

In reality, thirty is the golden age when you put life into perspective. Now, I know you're reading this and you're like, "Girl, you're tripped out! Thirty is old as hell! I'm in my twenties, I'm popping, I'm young, and life is hella lit! PERIODT!" Touche'. I won't and can't say that your life isn't the way you say it is. But, you're wrong. You're hella wrong. Yes, *hella wrong.* Now, don't get defensive with the truth. The truth is what we will encounter and accept along this journey. You will learn to accept the truth for what it is--nothing more and definitely nothing less.

The Question

I know you're wanting to know how right now. How am I wrong about my perception of *my* life. Why should I be "Ready to Be Thirty?" Out of every age... thirty. Don't trip. I'm going to tell you. First, we must dig into the root cause of why you even have that horrific perception of the age thirty in the first place. All our lives people have asked us the grand question, "Where do you see yourself in five to ten years?" They asked that question all throughout grade school by our teachers. I know you remember your answers, too! If you're a woman, you said, "I see myself married with kids, living in my dream home, driving a nice car, and working at my dream job." If you are a man, your answer was: "I see myself rich, living in a mansion with three cars and a baddie on my side." Typical responses for the sexes. Thing is, however, you grew up. You've aged, you've experienced life, and now you see that your life isn't the picture you painted for yourself. You answered that question and you were one-hundred percent sure that you would stand by it and live that life! That was the only life you set out to live, right? You would be that classmate that went on with their life and made that response become your reality. There was a lot of seriousness in the question. You *had* to know what you wanted out of life before you graduated high school! If you didn't, you were a waste, lazy, and didn't care about life. Period.

Twenty-Something

Fast forward and you're now in your mid-twenties. You are reflecting on that question, realizing that, right now, you are living in that five to ten years. It's sinking in that you are not married and you don't have any kids. You're not rich. You barely have a vehicle. You're living with your parents or in an overpriced apartment working hard to make ends meet. Your life is *not* living up to the response you gave when you were younger. You are not where you want to be: nowhere even close to it. You avoid your high school classmates and teachers. Who wants to give the rundown of where you're at in life when it's not what you set out for because we all shared our answers in class and everyone knows what you said in response to the infamous question, "Where do you see yourself in five to ten years?" You tune in on social media, seeing everyone living their best life thus far. Trip after trip, post after post, car after car, engagement after engagement: it's all draining and depressing for you because you're in your mid-twenties and you're not there yet. You're not anywhere you said you would be. So, you beat yourself up about it. You're angry and frustrated with life itself. You wonder, will you ever even get there? You allow your thoughts to get the best of you in the worst way, dwelling on where you could or *should* be in life. Where's my husband or wife? Where is my nice vehicle? Where are my six figures? However, you're forgetting a major factor: that you're only twenty-something.

The Pressure

You are in the period of life where you're figuring it all out. You are learning who you are as a person. You're learning what you like and don't like, what you want out of life itself, how you're going to get there. You are in the trial-and-error stage of life--the most frustrating and annoying time of your life. You try and you fail. You attempt again, but in a new way. You don't like the outcome, but it was better than the last time. When will you get it just right? How long do you have to keep giving your all just to get the outcome you didn't expect? Those twenties can make you or break you. There is so much pressure put on you by family members, friends, mentors, and even yourself. The pressure is real and you feel like you're sinking deeper and deeper into a place of no return. I can remember a time in my early twenties where I was in a deep depressed state. No one knew where I was mentally because, outside of my room, I put on a massive façade. I was down and out because I didn't have it all figured out. In my mind, I was in my twenties! I should have my career by now, be engaged or even married, living in a nice home with at least a puppy if not a child. Instead, I was living in a dormitory, single, struggling to pass my classes, broke, and having to fake like everything was okay. One day, I realized that I was only twenty-something! I'm still figuring it all out and that's okay. There's nothing wrong with not having it all together. I still have time. This is my time to make my mistakes and learn from them. Now is my time to learn about me! It is seriously okay that I'm not where my mind feels I need to be.

Just...keep...going. Be patient!

Chapter Two

Patience Is a Virtue

Being patient is a key factor in this process. Just sit back, keep grinding (put forth the action that it takes to attain success), and everything will fall into place. Right? We all know that's easier said than done. Being patient takes a special skill. It takes a plethora of self-discipline and self-reevaluating especially when you are extremely anxious about where you want to be in life. You can't wait until you've reached your goal! You imagine the feeling you're going to feel almost daily. You picture your reaction and dream about it often. You just can't wait to get there! It seems like it's taking forever and a day: time isn't moving fast enough for you. Being patient is harder than you've ever known it to be. Now you're wondering why: why is it even harder to endure this go around. I should be able to handle a little lag in life, right? I'm an adult. This should be nothing. Well, let me pass along some great advice that I was given in my early twenties: "Praying for something and then worrying after your prayer is only a slap in the face to God". Once you've prayed about a certain situation, you have given that all to

God, who is ultimately in control anyway. Yes, we have these plans in our heads about how our life is going to go, but if your plan doesn't align with God's plan for your life, then it won't suffice. God's plan is always the better plan. That's a *fact*. You have to trust in your prayers and, most importantly, trust in God that he will deliver. No matter how long it seems to be taking, know that your clock is ticking at a just right speed. You have to be patient with yourself, which is the hardest part of life.

Addressing You

We tend to have more patience with the people around us than we do with ourselves. It's easy to forgive someone for their wrongdoings than it is to forgive yourself. You know better, right? You can't find an understanding of why you allowed yourself to mess up like you did. You don't get why you're still making mistakes. Therefore, you beat yourself up because you know that you are capable of getting it together. You are equipped to do right and do right the first time, but you keep messing up. You are overly upset and you've reached the point of exhaustion and anger with yourself. There's nothing more hurtful than being utterly pissed off at yourself. You have to see *you* every day. You can't avoid you and leave the problem floating in the air. You have to confront yourself and talk it out. There's no way around that. Having a heart-to-heart with yourself is imperative. It is tough and scary, yet so rewarding when done. You have to talk it out with yourself and get an understanding. Have a sit down with yourself and get to the root cause of (and I'll be quite frank here) your fuck-ups. Look at the inner you and figure out what you need to change in order to grow up and grow out. What do you need to assess? How will you assess it? What steps will you take to go about doing so? Self-assess yourself to the core. This is a very important part of the journey to thirty. You have to be able to stop and look to yourself when there is a problem. You have to be able to hold yourself accountable for what goes on in your life. It's easy to place the blame on others and look at yourself as if you did no wrong. That must end--*now.* When you can look at yourself and say, "I am a part of the problem. I am going to change so that I can grow. I am going to work on me. Most importantly, I am going to be patient with myself." When you do this, you are one step closer to becoming the person you need to be.

You Have to Mean It

When you tell yourself these affirmations, the most important task you have to do is mean it. There is no point in speaking life into yourself if you don't mean it deep down in your soul. You are only wasting your time and time cannot be wasted. That's *not* an option at all. "Aint" nobody got time to waste. When you address yourself, you have to mean it all within your soul. You have to put in the work also. That goes with everything in life: not just correcting yourself. Men, you can't expect to reach success while sitting around playing Fortnite and 2K all day. Ladies, you can't expect to reach success by thinking it'll all be handed to you because you're beautiful or you have a nice body. Get out of that damn chair, put the controller down, and put in the work! Get out of the mindset that everything will be easy and it'll be handed to you! You have to put in the work. You have to feel it and have a desire to accomplish what you set your mind to. No matter what road block you face you have to keep pushing. Hard work never goes unnoticed, but no work is never seen.

Work for It

I can remember having that eye-opening moment in my life. I realized that life wasn't like high school where I didn't have to work really hard to achieve anything. I was called an "overachiever" in high school on a daily. Yet, I never tried hard to or be good at it. It all just came naturally. Of course, I practiced and I put forth effort, but not an extreme amount. While in college, I realized that life was not all that easy. I *had* to study! I wentinto college thinking, "What's studying? Tuh. Don't have time. I'll still pass." My grades determined that was a lie. Those grades screamed: "You need to get ya shit together and fast!" I wasn't used to making poor grades, so that had an effect on me emotionally. At that point, I knew that I would have to put forth more effort than going to class and listening. I had to do more than expect and want to pass. The same energy I had in my thoughts had to be transferred over to my actions. Did you catch that? I don't think you did, so let me say it again. The same energy I had in my thoughts had to be transferred over to my actions. I can't stress that enough. You have to put in the work for what you want. You can't stop at the beginning. Thinking is only the beginning. Your actions have to line up with your thoughts. You want to work on your toxic traits? Do some self-reevaluating. You want to get to a point where you are not easily stressed? Meditate, pick up a hobby. You have to work for it and work toward it. Period! Never forget to be patient with yourself.

Chapter Three

Pace

The process of getting through your twenties can't be thought of as a speedy process. You won't get where you need to be financially, spiritually, emotionally, physically, or mentally overnight. You have to understand that it's all a process. It takes time. How long doesn't matter, what matters is that you never give up on yourself. You also have to remember not to look at those around you and compare their success and blessings to your own. That's the worst action you can do to yourself. You can't look at other people's clock, how it fast it ticks, and expect yours to tick at the same speed. Your clock ticks perfectly for what is in store for *your* life. That is a very important factor. You can't compare your progress to those around you. You are competing with no one. You are on your journey to becoming a better you. You have to pace your life and pace yourself. This process needs to be thought of as the crockpot method: not the microwave method.

It's A Process

You're hungry and you want something quick, so you grab yourself a pack of Ramen noodles or some leftovers. You pop them in the microwave and you're eating in minutes. You are satisfied, but, in less than thirty minutes to an hour, you're hungry again, so you repeat the same process over again. Now think about cooking something of substance. When you are cooking a meal in a crock pot, you know that it's going to take a while. You know this before you even start, but you trust the process because, once it's done, you know it's going to be worth the wait. Once that food hits those taste buds, it's on and poppin'. You can see yourself doing your happy dance while smashing your food. During the process, you get a little antsy, and your stomach starts to growl a little harder than before because you're hungry. You are ready to chow down. You can taste it, but you continue to wait. You are patient because you know it takes time. *You* are that food in the crockpot. You didn't come ready-made and you're definitely not minute-made. Becoming you takes time. Becoming who God designed you to be takes time. You are slow-cooking yourself every day.

Start Now

A very amazing friend of mine gave me some incredible advice while talking on the phone one day. He said, "There is no greater time to start than now. Now is the time to prepare yourself for your thirties. Whatever it is you want to do in life, *now* is when you need to start. You don't want to look back five years from now, wishing you had put forth action to get where you want to be." That stuck with me like Gorilla Glue©. It hit home hard because there were so many ideas that I had in my head of aspirations I wanted to do: so many thoughts and visions that I had for my life that I had not even allowed to touch the surface. They were just there. I would think of them quite often and the vision would grow each time, but I never moved on them. I sat still so my great ideas sat still with me. It wasn't until that very conversation that I decided to start now. I decided to stop wasting time. I realized that years had already gone by and I still hadn't done a lot of the goals I said I would. It ended that day. I remembered that "anything lost can be found or gained except time wasted." You can never get back time no matter how hard you try. Once time is gone, it is just that--gone! My stunning friend and I talked and he hyped me up. He was more excited about everything than I was. He spoke life into my vision so passionately--more passionately than anyone had ever done so, and I decided to just do it. I went for it. At that very moment, I started.

Chapter Four

That Spark

That all sounded so simple, right? Someone asks you what your goals are and tells you they'll help you attain them. They speak the goals into existence for you and motivate you like crazy. That motivation feeds your soul and you just get straight to the business. I know, it sounds like some fairy tale. No, your spark won't happen exactly like mine did. In no way am I saying it will. What I am saying is it can be just that simple for you. Your spark doesn't have to come from big, breaking news or something major as seen in society's eyes. It can happen from a simple conversation. That's it. No life changing occurrence or tragedy that makes you want to better yourself. Just a simple conversation on the phone can be that spark. A sign on a billboard could be your sign. Hell, you pulling up to Sonic to order yourself a double cheeseburger for the third time this week can be that spark. You have to listen to it when you get it. You have to receive it and apply it to your life on a daily. Not just for the time being, but for the rest of your life.

The Company You Keep

You will begin to see life completely different once it hits you. Things you thought were cool to do won't seem cool anymore. You will feel disconnected from people you considered your friend. People will begin to question you and your movements because they will be different from what they are used to. That is all okay--I promise it is. Your moves will attract different people with different vibes, different goals and conversation, different money, different energy, different everything! This is a pivotal point in the process of becoming you. We all know that old saying about the company you keep. You know, the one your grandma said when she saw you start to hang out with those "fast-tailed little girls" or the "wannabe thugs." The saying, "Birds of a feather flock together." That means that you're most likely doing the same thing like those around you are doing. Now, I know you're probably like "just because my friend is doing it or is acting that way, doesn't mean I am." True enough, it might not, but that mindset can be the very thing that is holding you back. Joel Osteen said, "If you're hanging around people that are not going any place, people that are dragging you down, causing you to compromise, or draining your energy, you're going to get stuck. You can't hang out with chickens and expect to soar with eagles." Every time you talk to that friend about doing innovative actions with your life, the conversation is dismissed. You're told you're trying to do too much or you're tripping. They're not your true friend. "You're going to become like the people you continually associate with" (Joel Osteen). With that being said, surround yourself with bosses. Not people who are Instafamous, but individuals that haven't received a check from it. Surround yourself with business owners, entrepreneurs, authors, teachers, or any other caring person. I promise you will see the difference in the conversation itself. Joel Osteen said it best: "Who you spend your time with will have a great impact on what kind of life you live, and there are people that God has already ordained to come across our path to help us fulfill our destiny--people that will inspire us, challenge us, and make us better. The right people have already been lined up, but here is the key: if you're spending time with the wrong people, you will never meet the right ones." Whew chile!! Did you catch that jewel he dropped? If you are spending time with the wrong people, there is no way you will ever meet the right people. You are not placing yourself in the position to connect and grow out, but in the position of stagnation. And remember, there's no room for that on this journey.

Grow Up and Grow Out

There will be a lot of sacrificing along the way. With focus comes deletion. You can't continue to do things that don't feed your soul and expect yourself to grow up and grow out. The growing up is done more willingly for most of us. We are all eager to grow up. When we're kids, we can't wait to become a teenager. When we finally become a teenager, we can't wait to turn eighteen so we can move out of our parent's house and have our own possessions. We all grow up. We have to at some point. It's the growing out part of the process that gets overshadowed. No one talks about growing out in life. Growing out of relationships. Growing out of friendships. Growing out of bad habits. Growing out of yourself. Those are the aspects we don't think about but that are vital to life. You have to grow out in order to reach your fullest potential. You can't move on to the next step without growing out. That friend that dismisses you and never encourages you: deleted. That toxic relationship you're in: delete it. Those toxic traits you possess: delete them. It's time to grow out. Anything and anyone that does not add value to your life has to go and they have to go *now*. Whether that be family, friends, your job, or a bad habit, it has to go in order for you to grow.

There's No Room for Fear

Growing out is not easy. I just stated that you should delete some of the hardest aspects there are to let go of. They are a part of us. It's hard to let go of the things we are comfortable with. These are our norms. Starting a new relationship is scary. Finding new, loyal friends is hard. Shining light on our flaws is horrific. Yes, these are things we don't want to do, but we must do them. We can't enter the next stage in life trying to get rid of the things that shouldn't have followed us that far to begin with. Remember, we are ready to be thirty. Everything and everyone can't come with us. Now is the time to release them. My best friend sent me a quote about time and it hit home: "Don't let the fear of the time it will take to accomplish something stand in the way of your doing it. The time will pass anyway, and we might as well put that passing time to the best possible use." That quote holds so much weight alone. We all fear time. We fear time being wasted and lost. Not realizing that living in that fear wastes your own time. Why would you want to do that? Let fear go and grab ahold to faith. Again, it won't be easy, but it'll damn well be worth it. You may fail and that's okay. It simply means that you are trying. You are putting forth effort. That speaks volumes. When you fail, think about what Will Smith stated: "Fail early, fail often, fail forward." Fail early as in fail now so that you won't have to fail five to ten years from now. Fail often as in do not give up on your goals, dreams, or aspirations. If you are failing often, you are trying. Fail forward as in when you fail (because you will make mistakes); get back up and build off of that failure. Don't let the failure knock you down: learn from it and grow.

Chapter Five

Trust God, Trust Yourself

During this process, you are doing a lot of adult activities, if you will. You are finding yourself, analyzing yourself, trying new things, breaking habits, and letting old qualities and people go. Remember that it is not all easy to do, but it will be worth it in every way. Along this journey, you must trust God and yourself. When I say trust those two people, I don't mean that in the simplest form of trust. I mean, really and truly *trust* God and *trust* yourself. Trust in God so much that through the process, even when times get harder than ever, you never remotely think He doesn't have you in His arms. Don't allow yourself to stress about anything because what you stress over today, God took care of a month ago. When you cry about something, know that God is waiting on you with blessings full of laughter and joy. God sees the bigger picture that you are striving to see on a daily right now. You have to trust in Him that He will get you through because He will. Trust in yourself that you have the strength to keep going even when you feel as if you can't. Trust that you accomplish what you set your mind to. You have to really trust in yourself, believe in yourself, and stick to your guns. Block out all negative energy and accept everything positive the universe has to offer you. You will get through!

Positive Energy Only

There is no way that you will be able to effectively move through this process with negative energy and negative thoughts surrounding you. It is imperative that you think positive. What you think is what you become. That means that you have to manifest your thoughts. "Manifest" means to display or show by one's acts or appearance: to demonstrate. You want to become an entrepreneur? Act the part, and walk in the light of that. You desire to become a wife or husband? Walk in the light of a wife or a husband. You want to become a billionaire, then walk like one, talk like one, and move like one. When you think it, you need to walk in it, when you walk in it you are manifesting your thoughts. Thinking positive and manifestation goes hand in hand. Your manifestation shines light on the thoughts you have. If you are walking around looking like a bum, that is exactly what you think of yourself. You are showing others what you think about yourself on the inside. Get out of it. You are *golden*! You are worthy. You are more powerful than you know! I don't care if you have to look in the mirror and tell yourself these words every day, *do it*! Think positive because, when you do, so it shows. I read a quote that read: "You have to watch your thoughts; they become words. Watch your words; they become actions. Watch your actions; they become habits. Watch your habits; they become character. Watch your character; it becomes your destiny." That's a jewel on manifestation in itself. It's crazy how the mind works, isn't it? It all starts with a thought and that very thought will determine your entire life. Watch what you think and keep it positive.

Mind Equals Power

You are the key to your success. Your actions, your moves, your feelings, your thoughts, and your behavior all coincide with how your future will play out. You have the power to prepare yourself for what is to come. You have to prepare yourself mentally, spiritually, emotionally, and physically for what your heart and mind desire. If those four pieces are not in tact and up to par, you are not ready. Making sure your mentality is in the right space is extremely relevant. Your mind is top priority. Your thoughts are created there and your spiritual awareness helps guide them and keeps them on the straight and narrow. Once those thoughts are created, your emotional state comes into play. Negative thoughts create negative feelings. Positive thoughts create positive feelings. The way you feel emotionally ties into your physical state. Your overall health can be linked to one necessity: your thoughts. The power of the mind, right? With that being said, there is no room for manifesting negativity into your life on this journey. The preparation has to reflect positive thoughts.

Action!

God has already mapped your life out. It will go accordingly as long as you take action. The secret to getting there is you. You have to put your mind to it. I teach a kindergarten class of nineteen students. Every time we begin a new lesson or start something that may be challenging, I get them to stand up and say, "I can do anything I put my mind to!" I tell them to put some "stank" on it and really mean it when they say it! When they do, our lessons goes very smooth. Their brains are open and receptive to learning. They *want* to learn. There is so much strength in behind those words. If you put your mind to it, you can get it done. Put your mind to work. Train your thoughts and make sure that your actions follow accordingly. The dreams you want out of life are tangible. You can reach your goals and accomplish them, too. You have to want it. You have to want it voraciously. When you want it voraciously, there won't be anything to stop you from getting to it. Nothing will stop you from walking in your purpose. There won't be anything that will be able to set you back from attaining your goals. Tell yourself that you can and you will! No matter what people may think or say. There is power in the words that *you* speak over your life. There is power in the thoughts that *you* have over your life. No one but you can manifest anything concerning your life's success. Claim that house, claim that family, claim becoming a billionaire; claim becoming a producer, a business owner, a choreographer; claim generational wealth and residual income. Whatever it is that you desire to be, *become* it! Speak the aspirations that you want in life into existence. Claim all of the positive beauties the universe has to offer every day. Understand that you are in control of you and your success. You can have anything you want. Think it. Believe it. Manifest it.

Chapter Six

Three Stages

There are three stages of your mentality that will help you attain a deep understanding of your journey, your purpose, and your success. They all intertwine specifically with one another. You can't reach one level without having a deep sense of the other. We are going to think of these three stages as the stages of life. You are first born and, when you are born, you are classified as a baby. You are at the first stage as a baby. You grow and you become an adolescent. Your mind reaches the second level at the adolescent age. Once you reach that level, you continue to grow and you reach the third stage: an adult. There are levels to everything in life. The key is to open your mind and let it flow. You have to become so in tune with your higher self that the only vigor you can do is gain access to your higher level of thinking. It is life-changing knowing how to think and how to process your thoughts. Anything major that happens in life was merely a thought to begin with. We're not in the business of leaving our thoughts where they're at. Like Jay-Z asserted: "Bring em out! Bring em out!" Remember, we are manifesting for the rest of our lives: not just in 2020! Every thought will come into fruition. We will all live in the days that we've prayed for. Now let's get into it!

Conscious

The first stage of thinking and life itself is your conscious. Think of this stage as being a baby. Being in the state of consciousness means to be aware, to be awake, and to have knowledge. You are awake in life. You have been born and you are walking on your path. You are aware that you're here on Earth. You are aware of your surroundings. You know who are you in a physical sense. You are human and you are here. You are alive and well. You exist in this world. You have the knowledge of all of these aspects, yet something still lacks within you. There is something deeper out there than simply knowing you're alive, being aware and awake. There is power in knowing that you are here. There are people walking this Earth that do not realize they are here. It's not because they're mentally ill, but because they haven't opened their mind up to receive that awareness. There is nothing worse than being here and not being aware. When you are not aware, there is no way you can reach your highest potential in life. There's no way you can allow yourself the proper preparation for the next step. When you are not conscious, you're only existing and not living. Once you realize that and let your mind flow, you can easily tap into the next level of thinking. Being conscious is one response--knowing how to show it is another.

Subconscious

The second stage to your mental being is your subconscious. In this stage, you are an adolescent in life. Your subconscious is knowledge that is concealed and hidden. We are calling this the adolescent stage of thinking because this is where we are aware and thinking, but those thoughts are hidden. As teens, we all had a tendency of hiding many responses including our thoughts and actions we did that we knew we'd get whooped for into the next year. Your thoughts are in its adolescent stage when referring to your subconsciousness. No one knows about them, but you. Your thoughts are flowing and your mind has opened. You are becoming more observant of your surroundings, the people in your life, and yourself. You are beginning to put thought into the knowledge that you have gained over the course of your life. Now, you are asking questions. You are digging deeper and analyzing what you know. You are monitoring your thoughts. Now, I know I've talked a lot about thoughts and how you think. Your thoughts are vital. It is very important to understand how serious of a role your thoughts play in your life. Without them, how would you function or make decisions, let alone learn and grow. Tapping into your subconsciousness brings about a new you. You are thinking which creates manifestation. We know we have to manifest our thoughts in order for them to come into form. I remember a year ago thinking and picturing myself being happy within myself, graduating college, working in my career field, and finding genuine love. I wanted that hella bad for myself. There was nothing else that I wanted more than that, so I created a visual (thought) of it. I wrote it down and I pictured myself living in that moment every day. Months later, I found a new happiness in myself. I began to love myself in a whole new way. I started working in my career field a month before graduating college. One day after I started my job, a man found me who wanted nothing but the best for me and still helps me create greatness for myself. It all happened for me because I thought it, I believed it, and I manifested it. God started showering me with those blessings back to back--no Drake affiliation. I claimed nothing but great benefits from the universe and I got them. Of course, it wasn't all peaches and cream. There were times where I thought I'd never receive any of it, but just as soon as I had negative thoughts like these, I prayed them off. We think positive in these parts! Just as quick a positive thought can be manifested, a negative one came as well. Manifestation shows no favoritism. Therefore, be careful, monitor your life, and think big. Put your subconscious to use so that you can reach the utmost, highest level of your mentality.

Superconscious

The highest stage is your superconscious. We are adults now. There is no higher level in a physical sense than that. Your superconscious is your spiritual law. It is the highest level of being woke within yourself. Now, when I say "woke," please understand that I am using it in its fullest context. Thereby, many people use that word so loosely that it loses its value. When we use it, we are remaining within the context of the word. You are "woke" when dealing with your super-consciousness. You know exactly who you are. You understand who you are and you know and understand your purpose. This is the most desired mental stage. Being in sync with your super-consciousness should be goals. This is what you should strive for daily--knowing and understanding life. You can know something, but not understand it. Think about math. There are hella math problems that we know and still don't understand. *To this day,* we still don't understand how it works. We know how to get to the correct answer, but we don't understand the why or why you have to take each step you take. Your life, your success, and your purpose will not be in the same category as the quadratic formula. You will know how life works, how to get to the next step, and how to keep leveling up. You will also understand and innerstand life in itself. You will be in total sync with your super-consciousness. When you reach this level, there is no going backwards. You have reached the top. You will reach the top. This is what we long for. This is what we want to attract our minds to: allowing ourselves to reach our fullest potential.

Chapter

Seven

The Sky's The Limit

There are no limits to what you can attain in life. When you think it and believe it, it will come your way. If you think all you deserve is a man who dogs you out, cheats, belittles you, but still comes home to you at night, that is what you will continue to receive. If you think that living off of a woman, being a bum, working at the local grocery store, and stunting for the "Gram" is life, that will be your life. Like I stated earlier, there is no favoritism in this. Negative thoughts can be manifested just as quick as a positive thought can. You have to place yourself on a higher level mentally and watch God bring it to life. When you do, don't be mediocre about it. Think as gargantuanly as your mind can think. Imagine yourself living the lifestyle your heart desires. I don't care what Sally Sue or Buddy Joe said to you or about you, you can get there. All it takes is a thought. It is literally as simple as that. All you have to do is believe that you can get through this one stage to get to the next. By the time you turn thirty, you will be so mentally prepared that there won't be anything that can stop you from soaring even higher. If you are thirty now and reading this, start *now*. If you are forty, start *now*. I am speaking to all that are alive and well. You still have time to get to it. Redirect your thoughts so that you can redirect your lifestyle.

"Keep your feet on the ground, but let your heart soar as high as it will. Refuse to be average."
-Arthur Helps

Be Receptive

Many times we think that we can get through life on our own. We can take care of ourselves, get ourselves out of ruts, and dry our own eyes with no help from a soul. I am guilty of this too and I am here to tell you that this way of thinking is wrong: *all* the way wrong and there's no right to it. You absolutely *do* need help. There is nothing wrong with that. I realized that this year: having someone who wants to help me that wasn't family. Having someone who wiped my tears away and never once told me to "stop crying." Having someone in my life that tells me, "you're plugged in. Don't worry." That showed me that it is okay to have help. I have a hard time accepting help from anyone even my parents. I have always felt that I should be able to make it on my own. I have always been independent and I have always been a giver, but I've never been quick to take. Listen, I am working at this so I can attest that it's not easy receiving or asking for help. You *will* have to receive it though. In this journey of preparing yourself for your next milestone, whether it be thirty or forty, you will need help. You should never be ashamed of asking for help or receiving help. Oprah didn't get where she is on her own: she had help. Every successful person had help along the way. Whether it was help in a financial way, cognitive way, or spiritual way, they got it and they received it because they understood that it was necessary to do so. It does not mean you are not capable. It doesn't mean you're a bum or a golddigger. It doesn't mean that you're a freeloader. You are working toward your goal. You are pushing yourself daily and finding new strengths. You are trying to obtain security in life. You are trying. You will get there. There's no doubt in my mind that you won't. Keep striving and reminding yourself that you can do anything you put your mind to. Your mind is powerful. Therefore, inform your mind that it is okay to accept help if you need it, but be mindful who you accept it from. Everyone does not have their best interest in you.

Protect Your Peace

Your peace is extremely important in the walk on this journey. You have to become so in tune with God and yourself that no one will even feel comfortable thinking about disturbing your peace. It has to be protected at all cost. Your peace to you is as an umbrella is to rain. If you walk outside in the rain without an umbrella, you put yourself at risk of getting wet. If you stand out in the water too long, you will eventually get soaked. Allowing your peace to be uncovered and unprotected puts your cognitive and spiritual being at risk of "getting wet." Water yourself, but stay dry. Now, I am going to say that again and I want you to really take that in and understand it because I don't think you caught that: water yourself, but stay dry. Nurture yourself, allow yourself to grow and bloom as a flower would, but stay dry while doing do. Negative people are rain. Negative thoughts are rain. Unhealthy habits are rain. Keep yourself dry from those disparities. Don't run out to the rain. Keep your distance from it. If you have to go out in it, be sure to grab that umbrella to protect you from it. Your peace protects you from the rain. While you are protecting your peace, protect your mind. Your mind believes what you tell it. Feed your mind positivity, love, faith, and greatness. Nourish your thoughts and let your actions flourish. Remember as a child that one proverb you were constantly told? Your mind heard it so much that you eventually came to believe. Didn't you? It could have been the most positive quality or the utmost negative aspect about you, but it was told to you repeatedly so your mind began to take it as the truth. Watch what you tell yourself. Watch what you allow others to tell you. Protect your mind and your peace. They are your babies. You have to protect them with your all. Choose you first!

Focus

Let's get into some truthfulness about this journey. Life won't always be simple or easy. In actuality, they can and will be hard as hell. You will go through some troubles that will make you feel like coming out of it is impossible. You're going to go through the mud: the thickest mud. That mud may be a spiritual battle or a mental one. Whatever it may be, you are going to go through it along this process. You are going to go through it simply because you are on a journey of bettering yourself for yourself. When doing such an action, negative energy always tries to come in and drag you down. At this point, you have to understand that what you can't handle, God will. It is your responsibility to get through your battles and come out on top. It is your responsibility to keep your head afloat and your thoughts on track. Anyone or anything trying to pull you down is none of your business. Your business is you. If your focus is aimed at fighting negative energy and people then you've lost the battle. Your attention and focus should remain on *you*. When your focus is on you, how can you know what someone else is trying to do? Keep your eyes on the prize no matter how foggy it may get. You have a purpose and you were placed in this world to walk in that purpose. Don't play games with yourself. Believe in yourself. Believe in your vision and take the next step to ensuring stability in your life.

Chapter Eight

Push Yourself to do Your Best

It may seem hard sometimes to push through on your word of staying focused and keeping your eyes on the prize. Giving up will seem like an easier option, but, in this case, can you really afford to give up? Would that be the best decision to make for yourself? No, it wouldn't. Giving up is not an option. You have to push it to the limit! I'm no Rick Ross though. Pushing yourself to do the very best that you can will be extremely rewarding in the end. Now, when doing this and giving it your all, you have to understand that your best will differ from day to day. One day, you may be in tip-top shape and feeling better than ever. On that day, you were able to really go in and push harder than ever. However, another day you didn't feel yourself and your day was a bit of a drag, but you still pushed yourself to get shit done. Even with you not feeling yourself, you still gave it your all. It may not have been as much as it was when you felt great, but it was your best on *that* day and in *that* moment. Each and every day, give the best you can give however much that may be. When you look back, you will be thankful that you tried your best every day and not some days or most days.

Take Care

In the midst of pushing yourself, life will get overwhelming and you will feel defeated on some days. I am here to tell you that there were so many days where I felt like what I put in was nothing and not worthy. I felt down and completely defeated. At that point is when I knew I needed to take a mental break. We all get so caught up in trying to meet deadlines that we set for ourselves that we don't realize that taking a break is okay. Well, I here to tell you that it is. It is perfectly fine to take a break. Even more so, it is necessary to take a break. Whether it be a break for your mental health, spiritual health, or even your physical health. You have to keep those aspects in good health along this journey. There should be no shame in doing so either. Everyone needs a break from life and responsibilities from time to time. What you do with those breaks is what matters the most. For whatever reason you take a break, you have to focus on rebooting what has been drained. If your mental is drained, focus on self-peace. Meditate more often, sleep a little longer than normal, take a walk in the park, spend some time alone. If your spiritual health is under attack, pray. Pray that whatever is trying to gain your focus is released and binded. Believe that God will handle it and keep moving. If your break is due to the need of physical relaxation, just rest. No working out, no hard labor, and nothing that will put a strain on your physical health. You absolutely have to take care of yourself. During your break, gather yourself and get back to you. Get all of the strength you need to push harder. Taking breaks are a necessity; however, there is a very important factor to keep in mind about taking them. You can't let yourself get stuck in the rut that you are in while taking your break. You have to get in, regroup, and get out. Don't take a break and wake up like a bear coming out of hibernation only to realize that you missed the entire winter. A couple of days should suffice in getting you back to your regularly scheduled program.

Out of Sight

Many people have a tendency of publicizing their pain. Now don't get me wrong, there is nothing wrong with being transparent. If you are living your life in the public eye, by all means necessary, do you, 'boo boo'. What I am here to say is: you should not publicize your pain and hardships until you've gone through them and come out stronger. You have to realize that there are a lot of people in this world that pray on your downfall. Think about it this way: your morning starts off rough so you decide to post about it on social media and you deem it to be an atrocious day. You just gave one out of ten people ammunition to pray that your day gets even worse than what it already is. You made them aware that you were down and you gave them straight gun fire to light you up: this is what we don't want to happen. Don't give your haters or your naysayers anything to gas up on in attempt to stop your grind or your happy train. Stay out of the way especially when you are down. When you get yourself together, there's nothing wrong with sharing your shortcomings with the public. I actually encourage you to do so being that you may help someone who is going through hard times in their life. People need to see that other people struggle and have hard times in life just like them. They need to see that you can go through the thickest mud and come out clean when hard work and dedication are put into play. They need to be made aware of success stories. You just have to protect yourself when you are going through so that when you get through, you'll have a story to tell. Along my process of writing this book, I slipped into a pessimistic state of mind. I lost my spark and was having a hard time finding it. In return, I deleted my Facebook account. I did this because I knew that I had been utilizing the app way too much, but more so because I found myself comparing my life to others' lives on Facebook which is extremely unhealthy. I found myself wanting to tell the world how down and miserable I was feeling instead of going to the source: God. Therefore, I deleted my Facebook account in order to allow myself more time with God and myself. It helped out tremendously. I used my time more wisely, I began to pray more, I began to think about more positivity, and I learned a lot more about myself and self-control.

Don't Lose Your Valuables

Michelle Obama said it best: "instead of letting your hardships and failures discourage you or exhaust you, let them inspire you. Let them make you even hungrier to succeed." Listen, I'm not Waka Flocka Flame, but you should always let your hardships be the very reason while you go hard in the paint. When I say hard in the paint, I mean just that. Mix it up, splash it around, and create something boldly out of nothing. You may think that because you are down and at your lowest that you don't have anything to lose but you do. You are in the position to where if you don't make a move, you risk losing the most valuable movements in your life. Those valuables are: yourself, your pride, your dignity, your strength, and your power. Notice that none of these pieces are materialistic. They are all figurative aspects, but they are the most important. It is far harder to come back from losing those qualities than it is to come back from losing a house, a car, a job, or anything else that does not define who you are. Keep yourself grounded and focused at all times: so focused that when you fail, you don't even see the failure. It's a blur and all you see is you winning because your vision is solely on the bigger picture: God's plan.

Chapter Nine

The Series

During the time, I slipped into a negative state of mind and there was one major livelihood I did that helped me get back on track mentally. I knew that I needed to allow God to speak to me somehow. I didn't know how he would speak to me, or who or what he would speak to me through. I prayed and he led me to YouTube. There was this pastor that preaches in a way we can all understand. He relates the message to knowledge we can understand and relate to. His videos kept popping up on social media when I would scroll. My sister had previously sent me a clip of one of his sermons and I really took a lot from it. God led me to his YouTube page where there are a plethora of sermons that cover different topics. Now, in the state I was in, I felt like God kept telling me to go back to the beginning. Get to the root. Therefore, I went all the way back to the very first sermon that was uploaded onto the church's YouTube page. The series was entitled "The Expect Effect." I did not know what I would get from this sermon series initially, but, in the end, I gathered a lot of helpful and essential information that I tied into how I operate in my daily life. The sermon series was sectioned off into three different parts: "Faith It," "Believe It," and "Expect It." I will explain to you what I took from this and how it helped me look at life differently. Although I will be explaining my take away thoughts, I advise everyone who's reading this to go and watch this sermon series for themselves: https://www.youtube.com/watch?v=-19-VaWDRmM. You may catch something I missed or God may speak to you in a completely different way.

Faith It

The first part was titled "Faith It." There was so much information that I took from this section alone. I will start by saying the faith you have in God throughout this process needs to be fully loaded. You have to have that much confidence in everything working out for you just the way he intends it to because it *will*. Only if *you* have faith that it will. The more faith you put it in, the better your results will be. I'm no preacher or Bible expert and, no, I haven't read it in its entirety, but I do know that it purports: "... if you have faith as small as a mustard seed, you can say to this mountain, move from here to there, and it will move. Nothing will be impossible for you." That's basically stating that, if you have just a little bit of faith, *nothing* will be impossible for you. Thereby, you can only imagine what having a great deal of faith will do for you! Faith has brought about so many great magnanimities in my life. I had faith that I would graduate college. No matter how hard life was or how long the road seemed, I never gave up because I had *faith* that I would reach my moment. I pictured myself walking across that stage everyday until it happened. I had faith in myself and God to make my desires happen.

Believe It

When you have faith, you also have to believe in it like your life depends on it--because it does. Your faith and belief go hand and hand with one another. Look at it this way: you want to attain a million dollars in one year. You have faith that God will deliver and place you in the right positions to make that happen, but, in the same sense, you don't *believe* that you can do it. You want it and you have faith, but you don't really believe it will happen. Right at that moment, you voided out your faith. Your faith was cancelled because you did not have the belief that God would deliver on your behalf. There's no point in you even having faith if you don't believe. You have to realize that, when you believe great beauties will come into your life, you are making way for it to happen. You are blocking all of the negative possibilities out and paving the road for greatness.

Last

Chapter

Complete Control

Life is all about decisions. Your decisions are based solely on you: no one else. There's no one who can decide for you. Only you can decide what type of life you will live. The only person to decide how you feel is you. You decide what type of energy you give off, what you put in your body, and how you look. Your life and your life decisions belong to you. Ultimately, you are in control of you. Think about that for a second. Really grasp and understand that: *you* are in control of you. What goes on in your life is in your control. The good, the bad, and the ugly. It's all in your control. The decisions you make for yourself affect your life the most. Look at it this way: everyday you wake up, you have been blessed to receive another twenty-four hours. The same twenty-four hours, you were blessed with the previous day. What you do in those twenty-four hours is what *you* decide. If your day passes and you look back only to realize that you did nothing different than the day before, that's on you! If you look back and realize that you spent another day working hard and diligently toward someone else's dream, that, my friend, is on you.

You decided to make the decision not to pour into yourself. You decided not to change your daily routine. You decided to let another twenty-four hours go by and not attempt to find your purpose. We are all guilty of this. We have all let those blessed hours come and go and not put forth any effort into becoming who we are destined to be. We've all done it on multiple occasions. The thing is, that's another aspect you are in complete control of. When are you going to take charge and make a change? When are you going to decide that today is the day? Not tomorrow and definitely not later, but right now. Make it a priority to bring stunning energy in your life. Make it a habit of doing what it takes to get where you want to be in life. Habits are easily made, but they are hard to break so that would be a great habit to form: one where you realize every day that you are in control and you decide to take the next step. Watch how your life changes once you implement that one small step in it.

Take the Steps

I have talked a lot about manifesting and what it does for you daily life. Now is when we are going to take the steps in doing so. What you need to do right now is to close your eyes and think about what you want out of life. This universe has so much to offer you and, if you remember, there is no limit to what you can have. Think about everything this world has to offer and write down what you want now. It can be happiness, financial stability, love, job security, start your own business, to be a homeowner, or simply treating yourself to ice cream once or twice a week. What you want is what *you* want. Write it down.

What I want from the universe is:

_____

_____

_____

_____

_____

_____

_____

_____

_____

_____

_____

_____

_____

_____

_____

_____

_____

_____

_____

_____

_____

Now that you've written your life's desires down, the next step is to think about how you want to feel in the midst of it all. Close your eyes and picture living your life with the things you requested from the universe in it. Soak in that feeling that you sensed. Really get an understanding of what that feeling does for you and how it affects your daily life. Focus solely on those feelings and soak it all into your mind, body, and soul. Write those feelings down, now. Be sure to go into as much detail as possible about the feelings you want to feel in your life.

What I want to feel is:

_____

_____

_____

_____

_____

_____

_____

Antionette Turner

_____
_____
_____
_____
_____
_____
_____
_____
_____
_____
_____
_____
_____
_____
_____
_____

What steps are you going to take in order to get to where you want to be? What changes are you going to make within your life to better yourself? How are you going to make those changes? Think about all of this. Take these questions in and really think on them. What are *you* going to *do*? Now is where we take action. It's one thing to say you're going to do something. When you put forth the effort to take action is when you will feel nothing but pure joy inside. Thereby, write down an action plan. What will you do to change?

I will:

_____

_____

_____

_____

_____

_____

_____

_____

Antionette Turner

Now, you have claimed what you want and you've focused on how you want to feel. You have to understand that, in every waking moment, you are manifesting. You are bringing ideas to life with each thought that you allow yourself to think, each vision you allow your eyes to see, and with each feeling you allow yourself to feel. Knowing that you are in complete control of what you manifest in your life, you have to believe that everything your heart and mind desires will come exactly when it is supposed to. It will not be presented to you a second early or a minute late. You will receive everything you ask for and claim right on time. Be patient and let everything marinate. Let your request sit and soak so that when you receive the blessings, they will be good and ready *just* for you. Think it, faith it, believe it, manifest it, wait for it, receive it, and then live your best life with it!

www.ingramcontent.com/pod-product-compliance
Lightning Source LLC
Chambersburg PA
CBHW021157090426
42740CB00008B/1127

* 9 7 8 1 9 5 1 8 3 8 1 3 3 *